Inspiring

Teens

A Guide to Living Life

Without Regret

BY FRANCES VIDAKOVIC

AUTHOR'S NOTE:

INDEX

PART 1:

WHAT I WISH I KNEW AS A TEENAGER

12. LEARN TO LAUGH AT YOURSELF

13. PICK THE RIGHT FRIENDS

14. SAY GOODBYE TO FRENEMIES

15. DON'T DO DRUGS

16. DON'T BE IN SUCH A RUSH TO GROW UP

17. LOVE YOURSELF

18. DON'T CARE SO MUCH ABOUT WHAT OTHER PEOPLE THINK

19. RESPECT YOURSELF

20. RESPECT OTHERS

21. QUESTION EVERYTHING

22. BE ACCOUNTABLE

23. ASK FOR HELP WHEN YOU NEED IT

24. USE YOUR VOICE

25. LET GO OF FOMO - THE FEAR OF MISSING OUT

26. SPEND LESS TIME ON SOCIAL MEDIA

27. ONE GRADE IS JUST THAT - ONE GRADE

28. WORK OUT WHAT YOUR PASSION IS

29. ACCEPT YOUR BODY

30. BE CAREFUL WHAT YOU POST

31. WEAR SUNSCREEN

32. GET TO KNOW YOUR PARENTS

33. DON'T WORRY SO MUCH

34. STEP OUTSIDE YOUR COMFORT ZONE

35. STOP BEING MESSY

36. DON'T BE SCARED OF PEOPLE

37. UNDERSTAND THE DIFFERENCE BETWEEN THE "COOL KIDS" AND THOSE WHO ARE "NOT COOL"

38. RESIST NEGATIVE PEER PRESSURE

39. STOP DOUBTING YOURSELF

40. KNOW YOU DON'T HAVE TO PLEASE EVERYONE

41. TAKE CARE OF YOUR BODY

42. SOMETIMES LIFE DOESN'T GO ACCORDING TO PLAN

43. SAVE MONEY

44. KNOW YOU ARE NEVER TOO YOUNG TO INVEST

45. TRAVEL WHILE YOU CAN

46. LEARN TO PLAY AN INSTRUMENT

47. KNOW YOU ARE NOT STUPID

48. FIND YOUR INNER WARRIOR

49. DEVELOP SELF-DISCIPLINE

50. DON'T WORRY IF YOU ARE HAVING A CRAP TIME NOW - THERE ARE BETTER THINGS WAITING FOR YOU IN LIFE

PART 2:

WHY IT'S OKAY TO HAVE STRUGGLES IN LIFE

- THE VALUE OF PERSISTENCE

- 50 FAMOUS PEOPLE WHO NEVER GAVE UP
  CONCLUSION

INTRODUCTION

If you ask any adult what it was like for him or her as a teenager he or she will all have a different story to share with you. Some look back at those years with wistful nostalgia, wishing they could retrace their crazy steps. Others look back as if it was a bad dream, surprised to find they survived it intact. Whatever the case, this is your turn, your journey, your time to write this chapter in life.

Most adults do wish however they had had more guidance, support and encouragement as a teenager. They wish they had been braver and more confident. They wish they had been less afraid and more willing to use their own voice. More than anything they wish someone had shared with them the all- important words: like *"hey, please don't worry; everything will end up working out okay."*

This is why I decided to write this book - because there are things you absolutely need to know but you will never, ever learn it alongside Math and English at school.

And if you don't learn it from your teachers and your parents aren't so willing to share it with you just yet (don't cringe - one day you too will wish your sweet obedient child stays that way forever too) and your friends don't even know this stuff yet then it's up to me to share it with you in this book.

HOW THIS BOOK WORKS

This book is split into two sections. The first is WHAT I WISH I KNEW AS A TEENAGER. After extensive research, I have compiled a list of the top fifty things that adults wish they knew as a teenager. These are tips people feel would have made a massive difference in their life if only someone had shared this information with them.

Part two is WHY IT'S OKAY TO HAVE STRUGGLES IN LIFE. This section includes fifty stories where famous people struggled and failed often multiple times before achieving success in life. Why put this information in a book for teenagers? Well it's because I remember what it was like as a teenager looking at celebrities and adults who looked so polished and perfect. I remember thinking everything would be so much easier if I only was more confident, more talented, more – *fill-in-the-blank* - like them.

I didn't discover the truth until a lot later in life... these so-called successful people very rarely lived perfect lives. They had struggles, they felt pain and they were human too.

This section illustrates to you NOONE has it easy in life. So when you are going through your own struggles remember these inspiring stories. Hold on tight to hope, because there will be many moments in your life when you need something to hold onto.

PART ONE

WHAT I WISH I KNEW
AS A TEENAGER

1

UNDERSTAND THOSE CRAZY
BUTTERFLY FEELINGS
IN YOUR STOMACH

Teenagers are well known for their amazing ability to fall deeply and swiftly in love. You may have already felt these strong feelings yourself - the flutters of intense attraction, the inability to focus on anything except the boy or girl who makes you swoon.

Except of course we don't call it swooning anymore - the current term is something more like *crushing* because that is exactly how it feels. Your heart feels crushed, swamped, tight and sore - like a bird desperate to spread its wings except you can't fly without the attention of your much-thought about love.

I want you to know these strong feelings are perfectly normal and in fact they are to be expected during your teenage years. It is actually a pretty special and beautiful feeling. However there are some things you need to know about "love" before you decide to label the boy or girl who are crushing on with that tag:

- Love isn't supposed to make you feel insecure, ashamed or embarrassed to be you. It isn't supposed to make you feel like you are "not enough".

- Real love is reciprocated and generous. It is sweet and kind.

- People who are in love with you don't play silly games. They don't cheat or lie to you.

- They don't intentionally treat you terribly either or set out to make you jealous.

- Most important of all, they don't physically or emotionally hurt you.

- Instead they are respectful of your feelings. They make you feel valued, cared for and special.

For the record so many adults don't find this kind of love until they are in their twenties or thirties. So there is nothing wrong with enjoying the feelings you have as a teenager and appreciating them for what they are - fun and exciting, and something that will pass in time, even though it doesn't feel like it right now.

Just remember if love is making you cry all the time it isn't right. No person is worth your tears and when you find the right one he or she won't make you cry. You don't have to go chasing love – it will find you.

2

RECOGNISE WHO YOU ARE IN HIGH SCHOOL IS NOT NECESSARILY WHO YOU WILL BE IN LATER LIFE

In high school we are often given a specific role to play - there are the geeks, art freaks, jocks, losers, drama weirdos, goths, deadbeats, popular kids and whatever other label they have going on in your high school at the time.

If you can resist falling under such a label that is great but chances are it will be granted to you whether you like it or not. Now here's the thing - when you have been labelled as something (whether it's super nice or super suckful) it may feel like this label is going to stick forever. It may also feel like a mask you can't strip off no matter how hard you try.

For the four to six years you are in high world these roles seem like a division between the students. It isn't until you finally leave the fish bowl of a school environment that you realize these labels were arbitrary. They kept us locked in a box and misunderstood.

I want to assure you just because a label has been placed upon your shoulders does not mean you need to pigeon-hole yourself into this little niche too. Resist the label. Know you are more than a one-word tag. And guess what? Everyone else in high school is more than their one-word tag too.

Do your best to expand yourself and your friendships. Spread your wings by speaking to new people, especially those who are outside your social circle. Once you are outside high school you will be presented with and expected to socialize with so many different types of people that it is best if you are capable of getting along with everyone, sooner rather than later.

Stereotypes are fast and easy but they are lies and the truth takes its time. Deb Caletti.

3

LET GO OF REGRET

It's best you learn to do this early on in life. Things are going to happen that you regret. You are going to say stupid things or not say anything at all when you wish you had.

You will embarrass yourself, act like a fool, cry, lose it and not keep your cool, many times in front of strangers, family and friends. And it's okay because life is a learning process. We all make mistakes but we usually don't realize until we are older that these mistakes were actually lessons.

There is something to be gained from every crappy experience you live through in your life. So take the time to work out what that lesson was. What did you learn from the experience? What do you vow to do differently next time?

If you don't take the time to learn the lesson you will find it will repeat and show up in different forms throughout your life until the lightbulb finally goes off and you get it.

With age and time come wisdom and the greatest wisdom is learning to let go of regret as it serves no purpose except to make you feel guilty and bad.

4

STOP WASTING YOUR TIME
ON THE PS4 or XBOX

When you are young it's easy to waste hours and hours playing video games. This is because life still feels like it is going to last forever. You feel like you have so much time to spare and you don't realize yet just how precious time is. Well I am here to tell you time is more precious than you can possibly imagine. One day you will wish you could get back all those hours you squandered away in front of a computer or mobile screen.

Those hours you waste can be spent learning something new, building or creating something special, just doing ANYTHING that feeds your mind, body or creative soul. Nothing you see or do on your Nintendo, PS4 or Xbox game is real life. It's just a game, a game that's so easy to fall into but when you get back out you have nothing to show for it other than lost hours of your precious life. So learn to make better use of your time instead of wasting it.

5

UNDERSTAND FAILURE DOESN'T MEAN YOU ARE A FAILURE

As a teenager failure often feels like the worst thing in the world. When you fail you feel like a loser. You get angry at yourself and depressed about the world. What if I told you though failure is a necessary step to pass on the way to success? What if I told you IT'S OKAY to fail and make mistakes?

The truth is failure is something you need to embrace in life instead doing anything you can to avoid it. Because this is how we learn – we learn from making errors and discovering what does and doesn't work. Try to find someone in this world who has never made a mistake in his or her life. I'll save you the fun of searching endlessly for a person that doesn't exist. We all experience failure and hardship. We all have good days and bad days. This is part of being a human and nothing to ever be embarrassed, anxious or nervous about.

6

BE BRAVE

There's a famous quote in a Winnie the Pooh book by A.A. Milne that says: *"You are braver than you believe, and stronger than you seem, and smarter than you think."* I know it doesn't always feel this way but this is something I wished I had to encourage to be when I was younger - simply braver.

Think about the things you could do if you were braver, stronger and smarter than you think. What would you do right now if you weren't so scared inside? Would you ask all those questions you think are silly? Would you try a new sport or activity? Would you stand up to a bully? The truth is being brave is something we all have the power to be, even though it feels terrifying at the time.

Even though it may feel like the most difficult task in the world I encourage you to take little steps of bravery every day. The moment we learn to let go of fear and embrace courage instead, we start to gain more confidence. And confidence is something every teenager needs to have up his or her sleeve.

7

DO YOUR BEST TO
MINIMISE GOSSIPING

If you didn't hear it with your own ears or see it with your own eyes, don't invent it with your small mind and share it with your big mouth. Unknown.

If gossiping was an Olympic sport there would be a lot of teenagers who would be score a gold medal in this event. So how do we define gossiping? Put simply it is when two or more people discuss information about the behaviour and personal lives of other people. Often it is done in a negative way, maybe to vent or complain about a particular person.

Now I know it feels like a tempting or natural thing to do with your friends. It may seem harmless enough.

But most of us suffer from guilt and stress after gossiping and the negativity of the conversation usually makes us feel terrible. All I can suggest is you do your best to minimize gossiping.

As the saying goes, *do to others as you would have them do to you.* If gossiping is something you would hate having done about you (and I'm guessing no one enjoys being the center of a negative conversation) refrain from doing it yourself. If you truly need to vent, confide your feelings to a trusted friend instead of spreading negative words to every random person in the world.

In the end that only reflects back badly on you. Besides if you are brave enough to talk behind someone's back then you should have the courage to say it to their face.

8

IGNORE ANY GOSSIP
ABOUT YOURSELF

There is a chance people have spoken negatively about you at some point in your life. Unfortunately people are quick to believe the bad things they hear, even about good people. Gossiping is ultimately never fun, it stirs up trouble and sometimes even has the power to breakup friendships so try to keep a proper perspective if it happens to you.

Remember great people talk about ideas, average people talk about things and small people talk about other people. You need to learn to develop thick skin and ignore the ramblings of people who don't matter to you. It doesn't matter if what they are saying is or isn't true. Eventually people will forget about the gossip (honestly they will) but they will remember those who stood strong in the face of turmoil.

In the meantime note the wise words of Dr. Seuss: *be who you are and say what you feel, because those who mind don't matter and those who matter don't mind...*

9

UNDERSTAND THE POWER
OF YOUR THOUGHTS

When you're young it's easy to think your thoughts are something you can't control. You can't help but think angry thoughts, right? You can't help but feel sad or lonely, happy or mad. But here's the thing – you CAN control your thoughts. Even more importantly, your thoughts are so powerful they usually manifest into reality. So you need to be careful about what you choose to focus on.

You are probably wondering, what does manifest even mean? It means your thoughts have a tendency to come true, if you keep repeating something over and over to yourself. This is why it's important to think positively. If you constantly tell yourself "I can do it" or "I will succeed" then the world has a way of listening and giving you exactly what you asked for.

Just the same, the world listens when you repeat negative thoughts to yourself on a daily basis. If you constantly tell yourself "I'm so stupid", "I'm such a loser" or "I can't do anything right" are you surprised when the world gives you those same experiences back? After all you asked for it, didn't you? *You told yourself it was true.*

But you can change this immediately – right now, today, by stopping the negative thoughts and focusing on the positive. Tell yourself great things; choose to avoid words or labels that put you down or make feel bad. The recipe is so simple: think angry thoughts and you will feel angry and behave in an angry way. Think happy thoughts and you will feel happy and behave in a happy way.

Thoughts impact feelings, which in turn impact your behaviour. The recipe is the same no matter which feeling or adjective you choose to substitute it with.

10

YOU DON'T NEED TO ALWAYS CONFORM

I know it's sometimes easier to blend into the crowd. In fact many people try pretty hard to fit in, by acting the same, dressing the same and doing their best to look the same. Except here's the thing: humans were made to be different. You won't find a single person in this world who looks exactly like same, thinks exactly like you or behaves in the exact same way as you (yep, even identical twins are different in many ways).

So don't feel stupid if you want to do something different from everyone else. Don't feel tempted to agree when you don't like what everyone else pretends to love. You don't need to conform - that is, do what everybody else is doing regardless of whether it is right or not. You don't need to give in to peer pressure, just to fit into a group.

The most courageous act is to simply be YOU. Even if it doesn't feel like it will happen, people will respect you for being strong enough to stand up for what you believe in. You need to learn to think for yourself at some stage in your life. There is nothing impressive about being a sheep or a puppet.

So learn to celebrate your individuality because this will bring your true freedom. When in doubt remember this wise quote by Kurt Cobain: *"They laugh at me because I'm different. I laugh at them because they're all the same."*

11

IT'S OKAY TO SOMETIMES BE ALONE

I'm not sure why but some people are averse to being alone. They feel like it's the worst thing in the world. They feel like being alone is the same as being lonely and that it's indicative of how popular they are or a tell-tale sign of how many friends they have (as if the tally is zero).

Well I'll fill you in on a little secret: being alone is indicative of neither of these things. It doesn't mean you are lonely, angry or sad. It doesn't mean there is anything wrong with your life. Instead it is your time to be yourself, without anyone else telling you what to do.

Spending time alone is a healthy and important gift you can give yourself – a time to rest, recover and think about everything in your life. It also gives you the chance to learn to appreciate your own company. If you make friends with yourself and learn to enjoy your own company you will never, ever truly be alone.

12

LEARN TO LAUGH
AT YOURSELF

Life is honestly so much easier when you have an ability to laugh at yourself, even if the situation doesn't seem so funny. Think about it: every time something crappy happens you have two choices - you can either laugh or cry about it. Me personally? Crying makes me feel a million times worse.

People with a good sense of humor have a better sense of life and every time you find humor in a difficult situation you win. Even if you think there is nothing funny about your life right now, that isn't what having a sense of humor is about.

It's about learning to look at things from a different perspective.

It's about having the ability to appreciate the funniness in any situation, even when it doesn't appear to be hilarious at all. Sometimes things are simply better when they are looked upon with humor rather than rage.

You will need to develop this skill at some point during your life, if you wish to stay both physically and emotionally healthy. The sooner you do so the better it will be for you. Having a good sense of humor has additional benefits, such as strengthening your relationships and gaining a more positive attitude too.

So take your pick: would you like a giggle or prefer to stay angry, cry or sulk for days? It's all up to you.

13

PICK THE RIGHT FRIENDS

Good friends are like stars. You don't always see them
but you know they are always there.

Friends are pretty important no matter what your age but they play a pivotal role in your life when you are a teenager. This is because they act as a personal support group, during this somewhat difficult stage. Your friends provide you with a sense of security and belonging. They are someone you can turn to when things get tough and it helps knowing you are going through similar experiences and feelings at the same time.

So what does it mean to be a good friend? You have to remember friendship is a two-way street and it takes time to build and maintain positive and supportive friendships. A true friend doesn't care if you are rich or poor, fat or thin, if your house is a mess and your parents are crazy.

They will be there for you when you need them the most and despite your faults they will love and cherish the time they spend with you.

Friendship means understanding, even if you don't always agree with each other. It means forgiving, even if you don't always forget. A best friend won't always agree with you to make you happy.

Instead they will tell you what needs to be said, whether you want to hear it or not. True friends say good things behind your back and the not-so-nice things straight to your face. They see the pain in your eyes while everyone else believes your smile.

There are some people in life that make you laugh a little louder, smile a little bigger and live just a little better. Cherish these friends for they are precious. It is also important to be a good friend to those who are special to you. Be trustworthy and help each other out, and you will always have someone you can count on in life.

14

SAY GOODBYE TO FRENEMIES

You don't lose friends because real friends can never be lost.

As you get older you will start to recognize relationships that are toxic which means they cause you more pain than happiness. These "frenemies" are people who make you feel bad about yourself. They put you down, manipulate you and exclude you - sometimes very subtly so hardly anyone else notices it but it is something you strongly FEEL inside. You will need to avoid any "friends" like this or learn to deal with them in a way that keeps you feeling confident and secure about yourself.

If you have a frenemy in your life it might help to have a conversation with them about the way they make you feel. Tell them what you don't like them doing...whether it's *"I don't like the way you always leave me out whenever our group is organizing to go out"* or *"I don't like the way you gossip and say things behind my back."*

Focus on their behaviour and actions, without attacking their personality and give them a chance to respond. You may need to let this person go from your life if they still insist on causing you grief. If this breakup leads to bullying of any sort it might be helpful for you to talk to your parents about it or another adult or friend you can trust.

Just so you know our friendships groups often change during the course of our life. There is nothing wrong with moving on from one friendship circle to another if you feel like your old friends don't have the same values and interests as you anymore. It's fine to make new friends, especially if they bring out the best in you.

New friends can be found in your class, sporting or drama club or at any other extracurricular activity outside school. Often these new friendships bloom naturally as we have a tendency to gravitate to people like us; at other times it may take some conscious work to find new friends.

At any rate as you grow up you will soon realize it is less important to have more friends and more important to have real ones. In life we never lose friends, we only learn who our true friends are.

15

DON'T DO DRUGS

Drugs are a waste of time. They destroy your memory and your self-respect and everything that goes along with your self-esteem.   Kurt Cobain.

Drugs are probably the scariest part about being a teenager because they are a) rarely offered to children and b) adults usually have worked out they don't need that crap in their life. So it falls onto your shoulders now to work out how important it is to stay away from things that have the power to destroy your life.

I don't think there is a heroin addict in the world that looks back on his life and thinks *"wow yes, that was the best thing I ever did, taking heroin as a teenager."* Or a smoker, dying of lung cancer, that agrees *"gosh, I'm so happy I took up smoking. I recommend starting from a young age."*

Or an alcoholic that thinks *"yes, it's seriously so much fun making a fool of myself, losing consciousness and sleeping face-down in my own vomit."*

Most addicts, if they could go back in time, would not retrace those steps because they know the pain, stress and heartache that come from being an addict and how easy it is to go rapidly downhill.

Unfortunately it is often a slippery slope from experimentation to addiction. A lot of people don't even know they are addicted until they try to stop and realize they can't. Of course it is your life and you make your own choices but I want you to be aware of this strong feeling of regret that most drug addicts feel. Drugs can destroy you, ruin your youth and bring you unhappiness, grief and sorrow.

The goal for most people in life is to learn to live a life that is free from addictions; a life that gives you a healthy body and a healthy mind. Some words to keep in mind:

I don't need drugs to get high – I have a swing
I don't need drugs to "get away" – I have dreams
I don't need drugs to laugh – I have friends
I don't need drugs to have fun – I have bubble wrap
I don't NEED drugs to do anything because I am above that.

16

DON'T BE IN SUCH A RUSH TO GROW UP

Your teenage years are that funny in-between stage in life. Teenagers are treated like children but expected to behave like adults. Juice becomes alcohol. Candy becomes cigarettes. Love becomes real. Timeouts become detentions.

Training bras become push-ups. Pajamas become lingerie. Kisses become sex. Bikes become cars. Everything seems impossible. We become something we said we never world. Goodbyes become forever and broken hearts.

Teenagers are honestly some of the most misunderstood people on the planet. One minute you are a kid playing with your Barbie dolls. The next minute you are carrying the weight of the world on your shoulders.

But you need to remember you didn't always wear makeup or straighten your hair. You didn't always care about what anyone else thought. You didn't always think boys were gross or care about popularity. You used to love school and thought everyone was your best friend. You were happy most of the time too.

Can I fill you in on a little secret? You have the choice and ability to hold onto some of that childhood innocence and magic for a bit longer. You don't need to be in such a rush to grow up. Once you are a fully grown adult that's it – you can never go back. You can never be that fun, carefree kid again once these teenage years have passed you by.

Instead of spending all your time online, hating life, focused on exams, bitchy friends and bullies, wanting to run away, crying too much, waiting for better days to come, you can enjoy your youth. You can see life as an adventure, appreciate the friends you do have, sleep under the stars, tell stories around the campfire and fall in love with everything around you without worrying about losing your heart.

There is beauty in staying young and free. So don't be in such a rush to grow up...

17

LOVE YOURSELF

If I asked you to write a list of all the things you love you could probably name at least twenty things. Maybe your list would include things like: Kit Kats, honey-soy chips, your cell phone, Facebook and the TVs show Jane the Virgin and Modern Family. It could comprise of any number of unusual things.

What most of us forget to add to that list is the most important thing - OURSELVES. We are quick to admit we love our friends or our family but for some reason we hesitate to confess that yes, we think we too are great.

Well I hate to state the obvious but you are going to be spending A LOT of time with yourself over the next many years. Yep it's true - this is the body, mind and soul you have been blessed with for the rest of your life. No one else can make you happy until you are happy with yourself first.

So it's important you learn to love yourself and enjoy your own company. Understand you alone are enough.

How can you do this? For starters realize how special you are. You are a one-of-a-kind, fun-loving, unique person with your own special gifts to offer the world. Love yourself and be less concerned with the approval of others. There is nothing wrong with being you. After all who else are you supposed to be? Everyone else is taken.

Accept yourself. Value yourself. Forgive yourself. Bless yourself. Express yourself. Trust yourself. Love yourself. Learning to love yourself brings you more joy and peace than trying to love someone else.

18

DON'T CARE SO MUCH ABOUT WHAT OTHER PEOPLE THINK

Here's another secret: the less you care about what others think, the better your life will become. Except here's the problem: even if you don't like to admit it, the way other people view you is at least a bit important to you. Teenagers are prone to caring a great deal about what their peers think about them.

During this stage in life we are particularly sensitive to our social environment and the opinions of our peers can sometimes matter more than that of our family.

It's human nature to want to be liked and accepted by others. But you have to make sure excessive worrying about this doesn't have a negative impact on your life. At the end of the day you have only one life to live and you are the only person who needs to approve of your own choices.

So it's up to you to decide what is best for you. You know what is best for you - they don't. People are entitled to think whatever they want about you in the same way you are entitled to have your own thoughts and own opinions. And what's right for someone else may be completely wrong for you.

So try not to care so much about what other people think. What matters most is what YOU think about yourself that counts. You will never be able to please everyone. It's impossible to live up to everyone's expectations so there is no point in trying to do so.

Why beat yourself over something that inhibiting you from living your own life? Why obsess about other people's opinions so much it stops you from being true to your own thoughts, feelings and personality? The moment you let go of this worrying and allowing yourself to be controlled by others you set yourself free. You free yourself to become the real YOU. That is all we need to be in life, instead of a fake, unhappy, controlled version of our true self.

19

RESPECT YOURSELF

In case you are wondering self-respect is defined as holding yourself in high esteem and believing you are good and worthy of being treated well. It is when you know you deserve to be treated right. As a result you do not tolerate or accept others lying to you, hurting you, putting you down or making you feel terrible.

The way you treat yourself sets the standard for others on how you demand to be treated so don't settle for anything other than respectful behaviour towards yourself. This is something that is so important for you to understand. In a nutshell: if you don't treat yourself and your body with respect others won't respect you and your body either.

Some words of advice with regards to self-respect:

- Never chase or beg for love, affection or attention.

If it isn't given to you freely by another person, it isn't worth having. If he or she doesn't see your value it is time to peacefully move onto someone who does.

- Don't ask why someone keeps hurting you. Ask yourself why you keep allowing it to happen.

- Respect yourself enough to walk away from anything that no longer helps you grow or makes you happy.

- Sometimes you have to try not to care, no matter how much you really do. Sometimes you can mean nothing to someone who means the world to you. When you walk away from people like that it's isn't about being petty or proud. You are showing yourself self-respect.

- Just because someone desires you doesn't mean they value or respect you.

- When you are saying yes to others make sure you aren't saying no to yourself.

Try to always remember this - you are worthy of self-respect. Own it. Live it. Breathe it. Understand it. Because others will always treat you with as much as respect as you show yourself.

20

RESPECT OTHERS

More talk about respect, except this time it is about respecting other people. Now I know this is a sore point with lots of teenagers who automatically ask: why should I respect anyone who doesn't respect me? That's a great and perfectly legitimate question.

Before we answer that I want to talk more about what respect means. Respect in this instance means showing courteous consideration to other people. Examples of respectful behaviour include:

- Showing gratitude when you feel appreciative of something

- Looking someone in the eye when you are talking to them

- Complimenting the achievements of others

- Asking someone's permission before borrowing or using something

- Doing what you say you will do

- Offering assistance to those who need help

- Being sincere and genuine with your words and actions.

- Using good manners like "please" and "thank you"

- Being a good listener

- Making sure everyone feels included

- Respectfully disagreeing with others instead of fighting and screaming

- Showing genuine interest in what other people are doing

- Greeting people you know with a smile and asking "how are you?"

- Not staring at people

- Respecting your elders and others in need – by allowing them to go in or out of a bus, train or life before you or by standing up and offering your seat to an elderly, pregnant or any other person in need if there are no seats free on public transport.

- Remembering to say "I'm sorry" if you accidentally bump into someone in a crowd or saying "please excuse me" if you need room to pass.

These are just a few examples of how you can show other people respect. So back to the original question: *WHY should we act respectfully towards others? Can we pick and choose who we are respectful to? And if someone acts disrespectfully to us should we even bother being respectful in return?*

Now is the time to tell you another truth: respect is something that says more about your character than someone else's. Most people think respect needs to be earned before it is given (which seems right in theory) but the truth is how you treat others says everything about you and nothing about them.

Respect is important because it shows you value other people as individuals, even if they are crazy, disrespectful or rude. You don't need to stoop to their level. You don't have to lower yourself to behave in ways you intuitively know are wrong and hurtful.

Take the higher road and rather than play the "tit for tat, you disrespected me so I'm going to disrespect you" game, be the smarter, kinder person. Do what you know is right. Just because other people have no manners or tact or compassion doesn't mean you have to copy them or act the same way.

That doesn't mean you have to like or hang out with anyone who disrespects you. You are allowed to stand up and say *"hey, I don't like the way you are treating me. It is disrespectful and rude."* It is all in the delivery. You can do it in a respectful way or you can do it disrespectfully but remember this: people who show respect to others often gain respect in return.

Show respect even to people who don't deserve it; not as a reflection of their character, but as a reflection of yours. Dave Willis,

21

QUESTION EVERYTHING

When you are a kid you believe everything your teachers and parents tell you. You believe them because a) they are older therefore b) you assume they must be smarter and always right. Then you reach your teenage years and it suddenly dawns on you - there are a lot of questions adults *don't* know the answer to.

Sometimes they tell you something that doesn't sound 100% right. Other times they flat out admit they have no idea or they act elusive, with a million holes poking through their story.

Albert Einstein said the "important thing is not to stop questioning". Questions wake people up. They encourage new ideas and new ways of doing things. You are at an age when you no longer need to believe everything you hear.

You have the resources, intelligences and ability to look for new answers, if the ones you currently have aren't good enough or lacking.

Even if you think you are right or think you know everything it is still important to question the opinions and theories of those who influence your own thoughts and opinions. The more you question the more you learn and the more you learn to make informed decisions.

There are so many important questions you can ask yourself in life. *"What is the meaning of life? What is my purpose here? What am I here to learn? How can I do things better? What is it I still need to learn?"* And of course, the all-important one: *"Why? Why? Why?"*

When you questions things you get more answers, spark curiosity in your mind and force yourself to maintain an open mind. Asking questions makes us who we are. Asking questions is how we learn things. Asking questions is what has helped science and technology advance so far. Asking questions is what helps people strive for happiness and for a sense of belonging.

So the next time you have a question on your mind do not keep it caged inside. Instead set it free and allow your mind to remain curious. Most people do not realize how powerful it is to ask questions.

If you want knowledge you need to go out and seek it; it will not randomly fall into your lap.

The future belongs to the curious, to those who are not afraid to try it, explore it, question it and turn it inside out.

22

BE ACCOUNTABLE

This tip is pretty simple: starting today you need to be accountable for everything you do or say. This means whatever choice or action you choose to take, you need to claim responsibility for the consequences that follow.

For example if you break something that belongs to someone else you own up to it and replace the item instead of making excuses, telling a lie or trying to blame someone else. If you forget to follow through on a promise you made you acknowledge your error and make it up to the person instead of laughing it off or downplaying its importance.

Here's the thing: you are not a product of your circumstances - you are a product of your decisions. This means when things happen, even if they happen by accident, you in some way contributed to the event and you need to take responsibility for your actions.

No one wants to see you pointing your finger and laying the blame on someone else. No one wants to hear you insisting it wasn't your fault - that someone else "made" you do it. You aren't a kid anymore - you are a teenager and in a few years you will become an adult.

SO YOU NEED TO START TAKING RESPONSIBILITY FOR YOUR ACTIONS!

Examples of how you can be accountable:

- If you ding the door of a car while driving or trying to park, leave a note! Karma has a way of catching up with you. You should never run (or drive) away from your mistakes.

- If you were supposed to complete a chore or had a homework assignment due and you didn't complete it on time suffer the consequences. You deserve it! Don't whine and complain about it. You need to learn to be responsible for your actions. That is how you will learn to do better next time.

- If you miss your bus or train don't ask your parents or friends to save you. Wait patiently for the next ride to arrive and don't expect anyone else to bail you out. It's time to stop expecting other people to rescue you when you are late. Make a plan to be ready earlier next time.

- It helps a lot if you have reasonable expectations about things. If you have a project due at school remember projects take time to complete. You need to plan accordingly and not leave things to the last minute.

This is the first rule of life: every action has a consequence. Some of the consequences are negative, some of them are positive. You need to understand you are the only one responsible for your actions – you don't want to grow up believing nothing is ever your fault.

It's also not only what we do but what we DON'T do that we need to accountable for. If you don't help someone in need you have to take responsibility for that. If you fail to stick up for someone or yourself that is something else you need to be accountable for. Do what is right and not easy. To know what is right and not do it is the worst type of cowardice.

23

ASK FOR HELP
WHEN YOU NEED IT

Our one prime purpose in this life is to help others and if you can't help them, at least don't hurt them. Dalia Lama.

Don't be shy about asking for help. It doesn't mean you are weak, it means you are strong, wise and speaks volumes of your character. It means you acknowledge life isn't always easy and we don't have to go through everything in life alone.

Everyone no matter how big and strong could use a little help sometimes. Sometimes asking for help is the bravest move we can make so never be afraid to ask for help when you need it. What are we here for if not for each other?

There are going to be times in your life everything feels hopeless. You may feel depressed and lonely. You may feel like things are never, ever going to get better. You can't see an end to the problem; you can't foresee how things could ever be fixed or go back to normal.

At this point it is important to ask yourself some questions:

- What do you wish was different?
- What is the hardest part about your current problem?
- How does it make you feel - mad, upset, sad, angry, worried, scared, alone?
- What else has happened that makes things worse?
- What could you do to make things better?
- Can you talk to someone about this?
- Can you reach out to him or her for help?
- What can you do to help yourself cope?
- Is there anything that has helped you feel better in the past?
- What could you do to take the first step forward?
- If you had unlimited powers to change things, what would you do?

If you don't see the answer yourself it is important to reach out for help. There is always another solution, even if you can't see it right now. Spend time with friends who make you feel good. Get involved in activities you used to enjoy. Speak up and use your voice. It is ALWAYS okay to ask for help.

Also do not underestimate the difference YOU can make in the life of others. Helping the weak and vulnerable will make you strong. So step forward, reach out and offer your help to others. Your words, your kindness, may be the lift they need. You don't need to have a reason to help people...just do it. People often forget kindness is free.

24

USE YOUR VOICE

In life, finding a voice is speaking and living the truth.
Each of you is an original. Each of you has a distinctive
voice. When you find it, your story will be told. You will
be heard. John Grisham.

So you have a voice but how often do you use it to speak your truth and share the thoughts and feelings in your mind and heart? I want to encourage you to be bold enough to use your voice. Listen to your heart and be strong enough to live the life you always imagined.

To use your voice you need to first give yourself permission to speak up. Be proud of what you have to share. Even if your voice shakes, even if you feel nervous and scared inside, you should always speak the truth. Your truth may not necessarily be someone else's - after all we are all entitled to our own opinions and thoughts.

But you need to tell your own story because no one else can speak it for you.

So listen to your own voice, your own soul. Too many people listen to the noise of the world instead of themselves. Use your voice for kindness, your ears for compassion, your mind for truth, your hands for charity and your heart for love. Be true to the person you were created to be, do it for yourself.

You have something to say in this world. Something so true, so real, so you that it will ring unmistakably in the hearts of all who hear it. Are you willing to find your voice and say it? Jacob Nordby.

25

LET GO OF FOMO

– THE FEAR OF MISSING OUT

Every decade or so a new catchphrase becomes more than just a passing saying...it becomes a real, tangible thing accepted by society as something that exists and that is here to stay. That's exactly what FOMO is - a now common phenomenon we recognize as being something inbuilt within humans.

FOMO, which is an abbreviation for the saying FEAR OF MISSING OUT is defined as the fearful attitude people have about missing out on opportunities they think will bring them so much joy. It's when we get anxious because we think something interesting or exciting may be happening elsewhere and we feel left out.

We think *why weren't we invited to the party? Is everyone hanging out without me? If I say yes to this invitation what happens if something better comes up?*

So how do you get over this feeling of FOMO? Because you know you can't live that way forever - always worrying and caring about what everyone else is doing instead of focusing on your own journey and your own path. FOMO makes us feel ungrateful for everything we already have in our life. FOMO makes us feel like our current life is "not enough" even though it is potentially wonderful exactly the way that it is.

Accept you can't be everywhere, at every event that happens in the world today. You just can't be. Accept sometimes you are exactly where you are supposed to be at this moment in life. Every experience brings you lessons, both the good ones and the bad. Sometimes you need to focus on your own goals and this may mean missing out on other things which will only distract you from your path.

Can I tell you what you are missing out on when you get obsessed with FOMO? You are missing out on your own life. Every time you say yes to something because you think if you don't go you will somehow be left behind then you are saying no to something else. And that other thing could be what you need - some quiet time or study, a break, or more time to focus on yourself and your own life and dreams.

26

SPEND LESS TIME ON SOCIAL MEDIA

In a world where everything and everyone is so overexposed the coolest thing you can do is maintain a bit of mystery.

Have you ever gone on Facebook to take a quick peek and ended up spending hours checking out hundreds of perfect photos and stalking random people? Or clicked onto a YouTube video (something cute like babies giggling with energetic puppies) and ended up watching dozens more unrelated funny clips?

It is honestly easy to waste hours each day on social media - WAY TOO EASY. In some ways the internet can be a great thing - people use it to interact with others, form communities and build connections with people who share common goals and interests. In theory it seems fantastic - we feel as sense of connection and belonging to our family, friends and peers when we use social media.

Then there is the downside. The more time we spend on the internet the more we expose ourselves to people who can humiliate, bully or stalk us. There is even the potential to connect with someone who wants to harm us. And suddenly what seemed like a great thing is not so great after all...

You will need to work out your own way to stay safe and protect your reputation while enjoying social media in your life. See it for what it is: a simple tool – a tool you need to stay control of instead of allowing it to control you.

For some teens however social media is prevalent in their life and it is more an occasional hobby. Instead it becomes an "obsession", "addiction" and they can't help but spend hours looking at their phones.

Here are some facts: even though you think you are "connecting" with others when you use social media, real connection takes place face-to-face or when you pick up the phone. Your life on the internet is NOT your real life. Social skills are crucial in the workplace but you rob yourself of the opportunity to build them when you spend more time staring at a screen rather than into the eyes of a fellow human being.

Consider taking a break from social media or limiting the time you spend online. One hour a day is more than enough to see and do what needs to be seen and done (probably too much). If you used to spend hours every day consider delaying your use until after you have completed your more important and urgent tasks.

Learn to prioritize your time. Try not to define yourself by what other people say about you. Also try not to be so desperate that you crave positive feedback from strangers or people you don't know or care for.

Finally I want you to note social media is the new permanent record. What you post never goes away - it will stay there in the land of abyss forever.

Understand people put their best foot forward on the internet and it only provides a tiny snapshot of their life. People post their best pics (after culling them from a hundred bad ones and filtering them to perfection) and these photos paint a rosy picture which never tells anyone the whole true story. Be less concerned with how your life looks to others and more concerned with how you feel about yourself.

27

ONE GRADE IS JUST THAT: ONE GRADE

When you are in high school grades mean a lot. You study hard in hopes of getting an all-elusive A (or even just a B). You stay up all night to memorize, recite, sweat and dream about whatever subject you are cramming for and pray in the end all the hard work is worth it.

While I commend anyone disciplined enough to work hard at school I want you to know something. If you received a bad grade – please don't stress. That was one grade, in one class, for one semester, for one year, at one school, during one phase of your life. It isn't the be all and end all if you receive a not-so-impressive grade. In ten years from now it isn't going to be something you even remember.

Sure it's never fun getting a crappy grade. But this of it this way - whatever you did this time maybe didn't work and it may be time to come up with a new plan. Maybe you need a new strategy, a new study partner or tutor. Maybe you need to study harder or smarter or do something completely different.

Either way if you didn't get the mark you were hoping for, pick yourself up and start again. No single grade is going to determine your fate or life. One grade is not worth crying or beating yourself up over. Honestly it's not...simply plan for better luck next time.

It is also worth noting there are a lot of successful people who didn't go super great at school. Either they dropped out or failed important subjects or generally didn't go well when it came to academics. So please don't worry if school and academics is something you struggle with. One day you will find the thing you are great at and once you find this passion you will succeed.

28

WORK OUT WHAT YOUR PASSION IS

Passion sounds like such a tacky word when you are a teenager because it reminds us of some compelling crazy sort of love and it is something we would never admit we feel inside. But don't freak out - being passionate in this context means nothing about loving someone else.

Instead it all about finding THINGS and ACTIVITIES you love to do. Passion is when you have a compelling enthusiasm or desire to do something. It's when you love doing something so much that, even if it's tough or tiring, it still doesn't feel like hard work.

So is there anything you love to do? I knew from a young age I loved to write. Other friends knew they were great at fashion, art, photography, helping or teaching others and heaps of other interesting things.

It's okay if you haven't worked out what you love to do yet. Some people finish high school and still don't know what they want to do.

For the record I felt that way myself as a high schooler because I didn't have enough confidence in my writing ability back then to pursue it as a career path.
So instead of studying journalism (which I completed a diploma in years later because early on I didn't think writing could be a proper career) I went to university to study psychology which was another love of mine, working out what made people tick.

If you can't figure out your purpose then figure out your passion. For your passion will lead you right to your purpose. Find your passion. Think about what you love to do because time flies when you are doing something you love. Anything that makes you get out of bed, that gets your blood racing and heart pumping is worth doing.

It is important not to feel discouraged by pressure from adults or career counsellors. You don't have to become a doctor because your father is one. You don't have to become a teacher because that's what your sister decided to do. What do *you* want to do?

Don't be afraid to follow your dreams, if you know there is something you want to do. Life is supposed to be enjoyable; it isn't just about money or financial success.

Confucius said choose a job you love and you will never have to work a day in your life. Our passions are our strengths so once you figure this out - who you want to be and what you want to do - you can make a plan to get there. People with great passion make the impossible happen. Once you find this love and mix it with enthusiasm this will bring about both success and happiness.

29

ACCEPT YOUR BODY

There is NOTHING wrong with your body, but there is a lot wrong with the messages which try to convince you otherwise. Rae Smith

One of the hardest things about being a teenager is accepting everything about ourselves: the way we look, our strengths and weaknesses, as we desperately try to work out our place in this large, crazy world.

When we are young we don't think too much about our bodies: it is merely something we are born into and we know we can't help its size, shape, color or form. Most of the time we love it without judging or overthinking too much - it simply is what it is.

Then we become teenagers and for the first time we are conscious of our differences from others. We hear other kids commenting on what looks good and what doesn't. We start to notice what society thinks looks good and what doesn't (often the same thing). And it suddenly becomes a topic of conversation, either in our own minds or among friends.

What most teens don't realize is the concept of a "perfect body" is ever-changing. Back in the 1950s the media praised the voluptuous hourglass figure. In the 1960s they loved the androgynous waif. Since then the media has swung back and forth from loving fuller girls to thinner girls, boobs to no boobs, the super fit to leaner figures.

All of this sends a mixed message to everyone who is made to feel like they would have had in "perfect" body at some point in time, maybe just not the one they are living in right now.

Thankfully we live in a time where we all know about photo-shopping. We know every photo of every model is edited until teeth are as white as can be, until their skin is cleared of pimples and imperfections so it glows and waists and curves are pulled in until they are whippet-thin.

These images have been altered to such an extent they are not even close to real. Instead they sell to us unreal ideals and impossible expectations. Do not buy into these lies!

Here's the truth: I think the perfect body is the one you are living in right now. It was the one that was given to you, that you will have for the rest of your life.

Of course it is up to you to nurture your body, to do your best to respect it, keep it healthy and feed it well but you will never, ever be able to step out of it and into a new taller or shorter one so stop dreaming you can make this happen. Your body is yours for life so love it, accept it and treat it well!

Another thing: body confidence does not come from trying to achieve the "perfect" body (whatever everyone thinks that means right now - because remember in ten years' time it will be something different).

It comes from embracing the one you have already got. The true essence of beauty comes from being comfortable and happy in your own skin. It comes from having a caring and loving heart. Real girls aren't perfect and perfect girls aren't real anyway.

Remember you are unique and beautiful. You don't need to be a certain way to be yourself. Accept your body as it is. You don't have to love every single thing about it but you do need to learn how to be comfortable with your skin.

Instead of focusing on the superficial things appreciate all the amazing things your body can do for you - breathe, move, repair itself. Your body hears everything your mind says so accept it, love it and happiness will come.

Take care of your body. It's the only place you have to live. Jim Rohn.

30

THINK TWICE BEFORE YOU POST

Once upon a time this tip would have been something more like "think twice before you speak or act" but we are now a nation that communicates more via social media than face-to-face hence the adapted title. The reason I stress the importance of thinking twice before you post is because things are now different from how they were five or ten years ago.

Once upon a time you could say something negative about someone and it would be forgotten over time or you could deny it (if you needed to) that it ever happened. Nowadays however, nope we are not nearly as lucky anymore.

Today photos and posts are more like tattoos. What you post online will be there forever; even when you die, it lives on forever.

It doesn't matter if you change your mind two minutes after posting something and take it down. Technology has evolved to the point where people can screenshot a picture or record the evidence using a different device to make a record of your transgression.

So think twice before you post anything. Something you think is funny today can be humiliating or stupid the next day. Something you write out of anger or sadness can come back to bite you in the butt.

Words, photos and videos of you can be taken out of context and twisted to mean something else so guard your privacy and reputation like it's the most precious thing in the world. Because guess what – it is!

We are simply going to have to get used to permanence of the internet. Keep private moments private. You don't want to be forever haunted by digital ghosts. Many teens are casual about what they share online because they fail to understand the true consequences of what they are doing.

Comments, actions or images you post online can stay online long after you decide to delete the material. You will never truly know who else has seen it.

None of us can comprehend the true power of the internet that allows strangers, even creepy people you want to avoid, to tap into your most personal moments and memories. So think carefully about what you choose to document.

Now the important question: what do you do if someone is bullying you online or has posted something negative about you? Firstly it helps to understand your rights. Cyberbullying is bullying that is done through the use of technology.

It is important to know each state and country has different laws for bullying and you should seek legal advice if you wish to prosecute the offender. Everyone has the right to be respected, safe, and free from violence, harassment and bullying. A life free from cruel, degrading or inhumane treatment is one of our fundamental human rights.

If this happens to you make sure you keep the evidence and screenshot a record of what you have seen. Don't feel defeated if the post is anonymous - detectives are equipped to trace IP addresses and will usually be able to track down the culprit. If you have seen something on Facebook you can flag and report the incident to their staff and they will take it down for you.

So remember: think before you type. Report any cyberbullying if it happens to you so someone with the power to do so can put a stop to it. Most important of all – never be bullied into silence.

Never allow yourself to be made a victim. Don't listen if someone says you aren't good enough and don't let other people's opinions define you or bring you down. Keep the faith and always trust yourself.

Those who are at war with others are not at peace with themselves. William Hazlitt.

31

WEAR SUNSCREEN

We will keep this short and sweet. Wear sunscreen every day without fail, even when it's overcast, rainy or cold – not just when it's sunny and hot. This is the simplest way to protect your skin. Regular use of sunscreen has been proven to reduce the risk of skin cancer by over 40% by blocking harmful UV rays from penetrating the skin.

It also prevents premature aging and keeps your skin looking younger, more radiant and healthier for longer. Trust me, you may not care now but when you are in your thirties, forties and fifties you will be glad you used sunscreen as it helps keep the wrinkles at bay. You may not see the damage now if you get burnt, but it will eventually come.

Thankfully most moisturizers now contain SPF15+ making it easier than ever to remember to apply sunscreen on your face. Remember to also apply sunscreen to all exposed areas when out in the sun and wear a hat if possible too. Daily protection from the sun is the best gift you can give to your future self!

32

GET TO KNOW YOUR PARENTS

Don't cringe! I know this sounds like the last thing you want to do. I'm sure you think after spending so many hours in their company you already know everything there is to know about your mom and dad. Well think again. Your parents had a long, memory-filled life before you ever entered their world. It is crazy to think you could fathom everything there is to know about them.

Once upon a time they were teens like you. They had their first kiss, first love, first heartbreak, first rejection, first job, first everything in life just like you have had or are about to have. Even though it doesn't seem like it, parents can be a wealth of wisdom and experience.

But they aren't perfect, aren't they? Do you want to know why that's the case? Because there is no such thing as a perfect parent just as there is no such thing as a perfect child.

They are going to sometimes (or often) say stupid things. They are going to give you bad advice or seem like they haven't the faintest idea what you are going through.

Nonetheless every parent wants the best for their child. They will be trying to do what they think is right for you, given the skills they have, even if these skills fall short of both your and their expectations. They are human like you, which means they too will have their good and bad days. They will have their own battles and problems to worry about.

Being an adult means they have additional responsibilities that a teenager doesn't have to think or stress about, like bills and a mortgage that needs to be paid, meals to be organised, a house to clean and children to raise. Sometimes when we are busy growing up we forget our parents are also growing old and they have their own dreams to chase and fulfil.

Even though they may not be perfect, even though you may think they are annoying or old-fashioned or crazy or too strict try to appreciate your parents. Never complain about what your parents couldn't give up – it was probably all they had. You will never know what sacrifices they went through for you.

Ask them questions as questions lead to understanding. Respect and honor them as they do want the best for you, even if it feels more like it's the best for them. Finally love your parents and treat them with care, for you will only know their value when you see their empty chair.

33

DON'T WORRY SO MUCH

There a good chance when you become a teenager the type of things you worry about in life will change. Worrying won't necessarily be a new thing because even young kids worry about stuff. It's just the type of things they worry about are very different.

A young kid's worries are: *"what ice-cream flavour should I choose: strawberry or chocolate"* or will *"Dora the Explorer be on TV this afternoon or will it be The Wiggles, it better be The Wiggles!"* This later becomes *"Will I fail at school?"* or *"Will I ever fit in with my peers?"*

Teens are well-known for worrying about stuff like:

- Body Image

- Physical Appearance

- Family Conflict

- Grades

- College

- Potential Career

- Crushes

- Peer Pressure

- Not being accepted

- Meeting parent's expectations

- Meeting everyone else's expectations

There is little point in telling you not to worry at all because it is a normal human trait to do so. Babies worry about when they will get their next feed. Kids worry if their toy truck or doll will be broken by the rough kid playing with it. Adults worry about their work and old people worry about dying. But I do encourage you to learn how not to worry SO MUCH about stuff.

A quote to keep in mind:

If a problem is fixable, if a situation is such that you can do something about it, then there is no need to worry. If it's not fixable then there is no help in worry. *Dalai Lama*

I love this quote because it tells us there is no benefit in worrying whatsoever. Can you solve the problem? Then there is no need to worry about it. You can't solve the problem? Then there is no use worrying about it.

People say worrying is much like sitting on a rocking chair: it gives you something to do but it doesn't get you anywhere. So do what you can to stop worrying so much today.

Sometimes it's as easy as telling your brain to STOP. Take a deep breath and understand worrying doesn't actually take away your troubles. To the contrary, it is a total waste of time and doesn't change anything at all. Worrying about things you can't control only takes away your peace and empties you of your precious strength.

Instead of worrying about all the things that can go wrong, think about the things that can go right. Think about the constructive action you can take today to make things better.

It also helps for some people to focus on one day at a time. Don't worry about things that are one year, five years, ten years or twenty years away. Just focus on making today the best it can be and you can worry about tomorrow the next day.

Once again if you can solve your problem what is the NEED of worrying? If you can't solve it what is the USE of worrying? Don't think too much or you will create a problem that wasn't even there in the first place. If you fill your head with worries there won't be room for anything else. One day you will look back and realise you worried too much about things that don't matter.

A MINI QUIZ:

DO YOU HAVE A PROBLEM IN YOUR LIFE?

NO → Then Why Worry?

YES → Can you do something about it?

NO → Then Why Worry?

YES → Then Why Worry?

The day you stop worrying will be your first day of your new life; anxiety takes you in circles, trust in yourself and become free. Leon Brown.

34

STEP OUTSIDE YOUR

COMFORT ZONE

The word risk probably sounds like a scary thing. It may bring to mind activities like bungee-jumping and sky-diving which usually don't feature on a teen's to-do list. But here's the thing – I'm guessing there are a lot of tasks that seem even more terrifying to you than jumping out of a plane. This includes: apologising when you are wrong, admitting when you made a mistake and telling someone your true feelings about him or her.

These all entail taking a risk and stepping outside your comfort zone. So what exactly is a comfort zone? It is defined as a space that feels safe, comfortable and requires not much effort from you to achieve "okay" results. In this zone everything feels familiar and not stressful at all. Now here's the problem...magic often happens OUTSIDE your comfort zone.

In order to achieve something different you need to be willing to DO something different. You need to be willing to take a risk and step outside your comfort zone, even if you are feeling scared or uncomfortable. I am not talking about doing anything that's legal or wrong (that's a completely different scared feeling, which rings like alarm bells warning you to stop).

I'm speaking about the scary things that secretly excite you because they take you closer to your goals and dreams. Like trying out for the school play, or sending your resume in to a magazine you have always dreamed of working at.

Or perhaps it's having the confidence to stand up for yourself or the courage to start your own little business. Or maybe it's even the little things like exploring your neighbourhood, taking a new class, reading a new book or speaking to someone new.

When you take these steps you have the chance to finally discover all the incredible things that exist in the world. So when the opportunity comes up take the risk! Seize new experiences. Get out there and experience the world. Or maybe you need to get out there and create these opportunities yourself.

What's the worst thing that can happen if you try? You fail or get rejected? Big deal! You will discover later in this book that the most successful people in the world endured failure after failure after failure.

You are still young and the world is at your feet. Now is the time to try and try again. Keep trying no matter hard it is and never, ever give up. Make a point to challenge or stretch yourself in some way every day.

If you don't you may regret it later in life - indeed most people regret the things they have NOT done rather than those that they did. You don't want to miss great opportunities because you were too busy procrastinating and umming and ahhing about something silly.

This is your time, this is your life and you are the pilot of your journey NOW. There's no such thing as a time machine so if you think that when you are older you will be able to travel back in time and take those chances again think again.

You will never have this time again. Instead of risking regret, step outside your comfort zone and say YES to any great opportunities that come your way.

35

STOP BEING SO MESSY

Teens are known for being messy and unorganised. They have messy rooms, throw things wherever and have a hard time finding things they have misplaced. It is definitely a stereotype - there will be some of you that are neater than others.

Ask yourself now - how many hours have you lost looking for your wallet, cell phone or homework book? Being messy makes us feel stressed and anxious. We all feel happier and more productive when we start getting our possessions in order.

So do what you can today to start being tidier with your things. As they say: tidy room equals tidy mind. Throw away everything you don't love or need. If it doesn't bring you joy or isn't useful to you now is the time to bin it. Nothing makes you feel more mature than knowing exactly where everything is.

I am not expecting anyone to be perfectly neat all the time (I know I am not). I am asking you to consider the value in tidiness. Your room and workspace doesn't have to perfect but it does help if you understand there is "a place for everything and everything in its place." Don't put things down "just for now" - put it back where it belongs.

Pay attention to whether being tidier has a positive impact on the way you feel, especially when it comes to studying and getting ready for your day. If it does make your life easier, take some time out of every day to bring your environment into order.

36

DON'T BE SO SCARED OF PEOPLE OLDER THAN YOU

When you first start high school there is nothing terrifying than the sight of all the mature-looking seniors strutting down the halls. In comparison you feel small and infantile. You feel like an ant that could easily be trodden on or swallowed in whole (if anyone was into eating younger high school kids that is).

When I was in middle/primary school there were rumours whispered around the playground about what the older high school kids would do to you if you crossed their path. The stories included flushing your head inside the toilet, which alone made a shiver rush down my spine. Those urban myths kept the younger kids in line and made the older kids seem fearfully god-like.

It wasn't until years later that reality sunk in - the older kids aren't that scary at all. You usually don't realise this until you are a senior yourself but it helps to learn it ahead of time.

Once upon a time the older kids stood in your shoes and in a few years' time you are going to look a lot like them too. They aren't going to hurt you and they aren't on a mission to embarrass you. They don't rule the whole school either, if that's what you are worried about.

So don't be afraid to smile or strike up a conversation with someone older than you. You should of course always be respectful - no one enjoys being bossed around by a younger kid. Just don't be scared - they are honestly too busy living their own lives and worrying about their own problems to be fussed about terrorizing you.

37

UNDERSTAND THE DIFFERENCE BETWEEN THE "COOL" KIDS AND THOSE WHO ARE SUPPOSEDLY "NOT COOL"

I won't even try to define the term "cool" because there is no universal definition for the word. It can mean different things to different people but it usually encompasses traits like confidence, effortlessness and personal style.

The idea of being "cool" or popular is often a teenage obsession but there is something you need to know about these so-called "cool" kids. If you happen to fall into this "cool" category see if you recognise the truth in the following description.

So what exactly is the difference between popular kids and the not so popular? Deep down there is no difference at all. Popular kids are the same as every other kid deep inside.

They are human, which means if they fall they bleed, if they are hurt, they cry, if someone close to them dies or betrays them they feel devastated and sad. No matter what your skin colour, sexuality, religion or nationality is, these are the universal qualities of a human.

There is a story behind each and every one of us, a reason why we are the way we are and think the way we think. Outside of school we all have our own worries, stresses and battles to fight. You don't need to be in awe or intimidated by any other kid in school because the truth is deep down they are like you.

They fart (everyone does), they go to the toilet to do number twos (everyone does), they have fights with their parents and siblings (everyone does) and sometimes they feel like they are not good enough (everyone feels that way at times).

It helps to understand people are more alike than they are different. Some people think to be popular is to be happy and that popularity will solve many of life's problems. But that isn't always the case - sometimes popularity is more about appearances and conformity and this pressure to act in a particular way can feel restrictive and stressful.

What's more important and valuable in life is having friendships that are positive and respectful. It doesn't matter if your friends are popular and cool or weird and quirky (truth is: we all have a weird and quirky side) as long as they like you for whom you are. This is another universal trait – we feel most happy when we are loved and understood.

So remember this: don't waste your time putting anyone else on a pedestal. This means treating others as if they are some magical ideal rather than a real person. There's no such thing as perfection, remember?

We all have our flaws and imperfections, even the so-called popular kids (if you are well-liked at school, you will know this is true). Sometimes the people we put on a pedestal are the same people who least deserve our time and respect.

You don't have to be loved by everyone but you do need to love and accept yourself, whether you deemed popular or not in school.

38

RESIST NEGATIVE PEER PRESSURE

To be yourself in a world that is constantly trying to make you something else is the greatest accomplishment.
Ralph Waldo Emerson.

So yep, peer pressure - it's something you hear a lot about as a teenager. It's the main thing adults want to protect you from and for a good reason. In a nutshell peer pressure can be both positive and negative. Negative peer pressure is when your peers try to influence you into doing something you shouldn't do. Positive peer pressure is when a person tries to pressure you into doing something that's good. In both instances it's when you feel pressure to do something you normally wouldn't want to do.

Peer pressure is something everyone faces in school. My advice to you is this: you need to listen to the voice inside your head that tells you the right thing to do.

When you say yes to others make sure you aren't saying no to yourself. Learn to think for yourself and do what YOU feel is right. Wrong is wrong even if everyone else is doing it. Right is right even if no one is doing it.

Trust me, it's better to walk alone than to stay with a crowd going in the wrong direction. Stand up for what is right, even if you are standing alone.

That may be hard to do, but sometimes hard is the choice we need to make when the alternative is worse. It helps to know what your values are.

Once you identify your values you can make a decision based on them. For example if you value kindness, honesty and respect, simply ask yourself if your actions are aligned with those values.

You are not in this world to live up to everyone else's expectations and other people are not in this world to live up to yours. So don't change just so people will like you. Be yourself and the right people will love you - the real you.

When faced with peer pressure or a compromising situation consider turning to the friends you trust the most. If you can't talk to your friends because they are making the wrong decision, speak to your parents or any other adult you trust.

Know this feeling of peer pressure doesn't last forever. By the time you are an adult you will realise how important it is to be a unique individual rather than a carbon copy of everyone else.

It takes courage to grow up and become who you really are. So don't underestimate yourself by comparing yourself with others. It's our differences that make us unique and beautiful and perfect as we already are.

In the words of Abigail Breslin: *Never let anyone try and make you into something that you're not. Remember what it is that you want, and always stay strong in that.*

39

STOP DOUBTING YOURSELF

They say doubt kills more dreams than failure ever will and I believe this to be true. Doubt is that feeling when you are not sure or confident about something.

Doubt is like a parasite, a negative state of mind that eats away at your confidence and makes you believe your dreams are impossible to achieve. It sucks away all your confidence and motivation so that the battle is over even before it has even begun.

When you have doubts you lose everything and gain nothing. So what can you do to stop doubts from killing your dreams?

Firstly make smart decisions that honor your heart, your future and your sense of self. You know deep down that you have what it takes for whatever it is you want to do. Confidence is a quality you can find in yourself no matter how shy, scared or uncertain you are.

We all have problems with our self-esteem at certain times in our life – that is completely normal. We all sometimes question our worth or abilities. Self-confidence however comes from within – knowing failure won't kill you; it will only make you stronger.

Know you will usually get better at things with practice. Confidence is found by taking small steps of faith and knowing you can truly accomplish whatever it is you want with persistence, belief and determination.

Start by acknowledging your doubt and ask yourself where it has come from? Could it be some of your doubts are untrue? Are your doubts reasonable or unreasonable? Practice letting doubt go; tell yourself it is okay to give things a go. Even if you fail at least you have taken action and have the opportunity to learn something new.

When you fail you have the motivation to try harder next time in an attempt to reach your goal. Doubt on the other hand stops you from even trying. Change the way you look at doubt. It is much better to try to prove yourself wrong and fail rather than letting doubt control your life. Don't let your doubts sabotage your actions.

40

KNOW YOU DON'T HAVE TO PLEASE EVERYONE

If you live for people's acceptance, you will die from their rejection. Lecrae

People-pleasing seems like a good thing to do when you are a kid. You are taught by your parents to always mind your manners and do the right thing. You are encouraged to always respect your elders and follow the directions given to you by teachers and other adults.

Of course you get rewarded and praised for this behavior so you grow up thinking this is a great way to be: always trying to make everyone else happy.

Now here's the truth: you can't please EVERYONE. Honestly you can't, no matter how hard you try.

By this age you should have a good idea of what you are capable of and you should know it is physically and emotionally impossible to do everything for everyone.

Learning how to say no is an important step on the road to maturity. It is paramount you know your own limits and learn how to set some boundaries.

Some words of advice to help you stop this people-pleasing behaviour:

- Stop right now and think about all the times you have done stuff for others you wished you didn't do. Not because you were mean, selfish or rude but because this people-pleasing behaviour genuinely cut into your own personal time with your family. Or maybe it impacted your ability to focus on your studies or your own dreams. If you know the right thing to do is say no then it is okay to say no.

- If someone asks you for a favor you don't automatically have to say yes. You are allowed to say you will think about it or you need to check your schedule first. You don't need to apologise or over-explain yourself either if you can't do it.

A simple "sorry I wish I could help but I unfortunately can't this time" is more than enough.

- Don't be scared to be honest. You shouldn't worry too much whether people will be mad at you if you say no. True friends will understand if you are genuine in your reason behind your response. You also don't need to allow other people's opinions of you rule the way you think about yourself. Not everyone will agree with you, approve of what you are doing or think you are making the best choice for your life.

Pleasing everyone is NOT your responsibility and thank gosh for that because the key to failure is trying to please everyone. Never live your life to make other people happy because at the end of the day you are the only one that has to walk in your own shoes.

Ultimately it's not about being who everyone else wants you to be. Rather it's about being yourself and reclaiming the control and power over your life. So when you choose to help others it's because it's something you truly have the time for. Do things you want to do out of love rather than obligation.

41

TAKE CARE OF YOUR BODY

It is health that is real wealth and not pieces of gold and silver. Mahatma Gandhi

When you are a teen you spend a lot of time dreaming about how things could be more perfect. One of the things we pick apart and criticise is our bodies. Now I'm going to say something you may not think is true until ten or twenty years have passed. We have already spoken about accepting your body, now I want you to learn to take care of it.

This is it: the body you were gifted with and a healthy outside starts with a healthy inside. Appreciate your body enough to move it instead of keeping it immobile and lazy, stuck in front of a TV or computer.

Appreciate your body enough to feed it well because good health is truly your greatest wealth. No matter what your age you should never stop taking your health and fitness for granted.

For the record you don't have to eat less to stay healthy; you just have to eat right. Being healthy and fit is not a fad or a trend; instead it's a lifestyle choice and something you do for yourself because it makes you feel good.

Teenagers are notoriously famous for eating crap – burgers, French fries, chocolate and chips. This may be fine in moderation but no one can get away with eating rubbish all the time without it having some consequence on their body.

One day you are simply going to have to learn how to balance the treats and "sometimes-foods" out with nutritious meals. Remember you aren't a dog so stop rewarding yourself with food. Your body isn't a rubbish bin either so stop feeding it with crap. Eat good to feel good.

Love yourself enough to live a healthy lifestyle. We often don't value our health until sickness comes which is why it is so important to take care of your body now. Stay active while you are still young.

You can do this in various ways - you can join a soccer team, swim, play volleyball or run a marathon. Whatever you choose to do now is the time to do it.

If you aren't into organised sports that's okay too; you don't need a team or gym membership to work out. If you want to run go outside and run - you don't need a treadmill to do that. If it's raining, wear a rain jacket. Rather than a stair master use a set of stairs. Get your own weights to use at home, go for walks or buy a jump-rope or some exercise DVDs. Try anything you think you may like!

Honestly if you have the motivation to exercise you will find the time to do it anywhere. When you lack the motivation not even a members pass to an exclusive gym will get you out of bed. Start slowly and do a bit every day.

Exercise not to be skinny but to be fit and eat to nourish your body. Our bodies are capable of anything. It's just our minds we have to convince.

42

LIFE DOESN'T ALWAYS GO ACCORDING TO PLAN

So here's the thing: life doesn't always go according to plan. You may have already worked this out in your life. Maybe you made plans to do something special with a friend and they ditched you at the last minute. Maybe your parents promised you a new phone for your birthday and instead all you got were some socks. All I can say is this: yes it seriously sucks but life is not always predictable or fair.

Sorry I know you probably don't want to hear this from me but it's true. Sometimes the best person doesn't get the prize; sometimes the pushy person gets recognised ahead of the nice one who waited longer and more patiently. Sometimes you get blamed for things you didn't do or you miss out on things you had your heart set on getting.

But that's life. It's unfair and unpredictable for EVERYONE so in a way that's the only thing that makes it fair (in a weird kind of way). Much better you get used to this fact instead of fighting something you can't change.

This is why it is so important to be flexible and to learn how to go with the flow. Often you will need a Plan B or C, or maybe even a Plan D, E or F, depending on how many challenges you end up facing in life.

Being flexible means being willing and open to change because life will never stay the same. This doesn't mean you have to give up on your goals. It simply means you have to be open to trying out different methods to achieve what you want.

Life is series of choices and changes. If you don't make the team, get the job, or pass a test, try not to stress too much. Your life isn't over...when one door closes another door usually opens. Sometimes good things fall apart so better things can fall together.

43

SAVE YOUR MONEY

One of the most exciting things about becoming a teenager is the ability to finally go out and earn your own income. When you first start working or getting an allowance I know it is tempting to spend it all in one go. So many shops and not enough time! For the first time in your life you are in charge of your money and that feeling of freedom brings you so much joy.

I know it seems crazy to think about saving for a new car or down payment for a house when you are still young but honestly this is the best time to start saving your hard-earned dollars. Maybe you don't care for either of these two things right now but trust me, there will be something you value in the future and you will need money to acquire it.

Want to travel the world or live overseas? You need money for that, lots of it. Want to start a business? You need money for that too.

Your parents may of course help you out with some stuff but there will be a million more things on your wish list you will need to work your butt off to attain.

So given you may want something in the future that requires a lot of money I want you to be mindful now of how you spend your pennies. Once you spend it you usually can't get it back and every single dollar you waste is gone forever.

Think twice about spending all your money on food, clothes and drinks. These are the three biggest money wasters for both adults and teens. Ask yourself: are the things you are buying meaningful or wasteful? Are you getting value for your money?

There is no rule that says you need to spend everything that is in your wallet. If you need to spend your money, use it on something that has enduring value. Otherwise save your precious cash for your future or a rainy day. You need to learn this lesson at some point in your life so why not now?

44

KNOW YOU ARE NEVER TOO YOUNG TO INVEST

Yep more money talk, just what you want to hear (maybe not!) Investing is something most teenagers never consider doing but guess what? Those who start young have the most chance of success. Investing is when you make your money grow without you doing much at all. You can choose to invest in property, stocks, term deposits or any of the other investment strategies that are available to you if you have the funds.

This may sound like a foreign language to you which is why you will need to do your own research first. Use the Internet to find out what options are available to you. Read books on the topic and ask any financially successful people you know what advice they may have to share. MOST IMPORTANT OF ALL - ASK FOR HELP!

No matter how much we try when we are older we can never get back that head start we missed in our younger years. So consider investing earlier rather than later in life. Later on you may wish you had!

45

TRAVEL WHILE YOU CAN

I know travelling is something you may not have the opportunity to do until after you finish school or college but I mention it now because it's the biggest regret noted by adults about what they would change if they could go back in time.

In case you haven't guessed it yet there is so much more to this world than simply the place where you are born. Outside our comfort zone exists an amazing plethora of different cultures and countries you have to experience to properly embrace.

Everyone has different places written on their wish list (my own bucket list included Paris, Venice, London and Barcelona while other friends of mine sought to explore Africa, Asia and the Americas). You will know what makes your heart flutter; it honestly isn't something other people can dictate to you.

Now here's the thing...we typically don't get the opportunity to travel until we are in our twenties but around the same time other priorities start knocking on our door: marriage, kids, a mortgage and a stable career.

Even though we often have the best intentions to travel, things are harder once you find yourself settled. So if you want to travel I encourage you to plan for it early. Don't leave it until it is too late. A lot of people think they will have time to travel later but do you know what? That is rarely the case.

46

LEARN TO PLAY AN

INSTRUMENT

If you have even an inkling of a desire to learn how to play an instrument I encourage you to do it now, while you are still young. Trust me, thirteen, fourteen, fifteen or even nineteen, is still young enough to learn how to play any instrument well.

Don't believe me? Then ask someone who is thirty, forty or fifty years old. They will tell you the value of having ten, twenty or thirty years of practice under their belt. The expert in anything was once a beginner and if you practice it regularly you will be surprised by how much better you get over time.

Even if you don't become a professional at least you will get further than someone who never got off their butt to try.

47

KNOW YOU ARE NOT STUPID

Even if you sometimes do or say silly things, that doesn't mean you are stupid in any way. To the contrary you are a young human being who is still learning your way around this world, like every other individual on this planet.

You are going to make mistakes - lots of them. You are sometimes going to be naïve and clueless about things but only because you haven't lived long enough to understand every concept in this world like some Brainiac college student or wise old owl.

So don't waste your time comparing yourself to others. Big deal if someone has achieved more in their life so far. Maybe you haven't had the same opportunities as he or she has. Maybe you haven't had access to the same lessons and information as he or she has. Your time will eventually come and when it does you will be ready.

In the meantime don't ever put yourself down if you haven't learned something yet. You aren't stupid if someone gets a higher grade or accomplishes more in their life. Maybe you need more time for the lesson to sink in. Maybe you didn't even know there was a lesson to be learned.

Everything happens for a reason and there will be times when you simply make a bad decision. If that's the case pick yourself up and move on. Just because you don't like where you have to start from doesn't mean you shouldn't get started. If you find yourself in a situation where you feel worried or feel like you don't know enough, don't waste time kicking yourself for feeling clueless.

Understand this: you are not alone. You are perfect even if you feel like you are lacking. Accept your feelings and appreciate your unique mind. Who says you have to know everything in order to be valued and respected?

Take joy in the things you do know - you have your own wisdom you can teach and inspire others with. If everyone had the exact same interests and knowledge, the world would be a pretty boring place. Feel empowered by what you do know and consider the only thing you may be lacking is some more confidence in yourself.

48

FIND YOUR INNER WARRIOR

Do not speak badly of your elf. For the warrior within hears your words and is lessoned by them. David Gemmell

I have already mentioned life is sometimes going to be tough. It isn't always a bed of roses or filled with peaches and cream. You will have days that test your strength, courage and patience. You will find yourself in situations that make you want to give up, throw in the towel or not do anything useful for a while. This is a fact of life. During times like this it helps to know you have an inner warrior you can call upon to help you out.

Your inner warrior has the strength, power and determination to tackle anything that comes her way. Courage above all things is the most important quality of your inner warrior.

Your inner warrior makes decisions that are committed to your dreams. It believes in miracles and understands nobody is perfect - not even you.

But that doesn't matter nor change anything as imperfect people can still live wonderful, beautiful lives filled with happiness.

You have an inner warrior living inside you - we all do. Your inner warrior will fight for you, love you and protect you so call upon this strength whenever you need it in your life.

49

DEVELOP SELF-DISCIPLINE

Discipline is doing what needs to be done, even if you don't want to do it. Maybe it didn't matter so much when you were a kid because your parents were always there to pull you into line but as you get older you will need to develop this self-discipline yourself.

For the first time you are going to be placed in situations where the only person you need to answer to is yourself. Like with studying – your parents may not be there to yell at you to get to work. Or with healthy eating – your parents may not be there to encourage you to buy a healthy sandwich instead of a crappy, preservative-filled burger. The choice will be up to you and no one else.

You need to remember being self-disciplined isn't supposed to be a punishment. Instead it exists to steer you down the right path. With self-discipline almost anything is possible. It helps to improve you and create a bridge between your dreams and your reality.

Ask yourself: *will this particular behaviour get me to where I need to be?* Think about what you want and what you need to do to get there. Choose what is best for you regardless of how you feel. If you are feeling lazy or unmotivated remind yourself why you are doing it in the first place. What is your ultimate goal?

Be prepared to face difficulty – no one said life would be easy. The real value of self-discipline is not in the reward but in the sort of person we become as a result as behaving in a committed, focused way. Self-discipline makes us feel strong and confident. Thankfully the more disciplined you become, the easier life gets.

We don't have to be smarter than the rest; we have to be more disciplined than the rest. Warren Buffett

50

DON'T WORRY IF YOU ARE HAVING A CRAP TIME NOW - THERE ARE BETTER THINGS WAITING FOR YOU IN LIFE

So here it is - my last piece of advice for you. They often say your teen years are the best years of your life but I know for some these words will not be reassuring. After all if you are having a crappy time now, does that mean there's nothing exciting for you to look forward to in life? Does that mean this is seriously the best it is going to get?

No way, absolutely not. Sure your teen years are fun in the "free from serious responsibilities" sort of way but the truth is it's the beginning and not the end of your life. You can expect many more enjoyable and rewarding things to happen throughout your life.

You are now on the brink of a new beginning with so many amazing things on your horizon. You will one day leave school, drive a car, have a job, earn some money, fall in love, own a house and have children - not necessarily in that order or all of the above.

How you live your life is up to you. Just because someone had a great time during their teenage years doesn't mean you will too. Or just because another person had a traumatic time during their teen years doesn't mean you will have the same. It is all up to the individual - no one lives the same life or has the exact same experiences.

It is helpful to know you can make your life awesome, fun, meaningful, and special at every stage of your life. If you didn't luck out in your teens don't worry. Plenty of people create fulfilling, happy lives when they are twenty, thirty, forty, fifty, sixty and above.

There is no age limit to happiness. Good things come to those who believe, better things come to those who are patient and the best things come to those who never give up. So don't worry. There are better things ahead than any we leave behind.

PART TWO

WHY IT'S OKAY TO HAVE
STRUGGLES IN LIFE

So you failed? Big deal!

Let's start this section off with a little story

Once there was a boy who met a wise man on the road. He asked him "which way is it to success?" The wise man did not speak but simply pointed to a place off in the distance. The boy, who was thrilled with the discovery of a short cut to success, rushed off in the appropriate direction.

Suddenly there was a loud splat. The boy, shocked by the collision, slowly picked himself back and staggered back to the wise man, limping, battered, and stunned. He asked the wise man the same question, assuming he had misinterpreted his previous response. But the wise man once again silently pointed in the same direction.

This time the boy was a little sceptical but he obediently walked off once more.

Then it came - another deafening splat and when the boy crawled back he was bloody, broken and angry beyond belief. He screamed at the wise man, "I asked you which was the way to success and I went the way you indicated. Yet all I got was splatted. Enough of this pointing business! I want you to talk to me!"

Only then did the wise man speak and what he said was this: "Success IS indeed that way. But it's just a little PAST the splat."

THE VALUE OF PERSISTENCE

Yes it sucks but it's true. If you were to ask any successful person about their secret, they would most certainly tell you it's "persistence." Persistence is what makes champions; persistence is what gets results; persistence means never giving up until you get your goal. In the history of mankind no one has ever achieved anything worthwhile without the ability to stay strong and endure the pain and pitfalls when they come.

Except persistence takes courage

One of the biggest reasons for why we sell ourselves short and underachieve in life is because we assume people who are doing better than us ARE BETTER. Yet this simply isn't true. If you take the time to study any successful person you will learn the vast majority of them have had way more 'failures' in life than they have had 'successes'.

People who are considered to be highly successful in fact only succeed 60% of the time. 99% of all financially successful people today began their careers either broke or nearly broke and the average self-made millionaire has been bankrupt or close to bankruptcy at least 3 times.

Successful people are not afraid to fail. They have the ability to accept their failures and carry on, knowing that failure is a natural consequence of trying. The more they stumble and fall, the more they get right back up and keep on going. Those who don't get back up? Unfortunately they never reach success.

Persistence requires faith

The world is full of people who "made an effort" to chase their dreams. However upon meeting difficulty or rejections they quickly quit and decided it is all "too hard". Yet why should succeeding in life be any different from learning to play an instrument or learning a new language? You need to have FAITH that you will eventually be rewarded for your dedication and effort, even if the payoff is many years down the track.

Of course you are going to stumble sometimes but teens that persevere through the stumbles - who don't let that stop them or impact their dreams - learn so much through the stumbling process that it provides the foundation to their success. It is simply the "sticking with it" attitude that separates those who succeed and those who don't.

Count on the obstacles

Too many teens make the mistake of quitting just short of success. But you should count on the obstacles. They are a part of life. They are TO BE EXPECTED.

Your job is to be persistent and work through the obstacles. If you find little or no roadblocks along your journey in life chances are you are not challenging yourself. Make your goals challenging ones.

Falling down is inevitable

It helps if you understand falling down comes with the territory of trying to accomplish a difficult task. It's okay if you fall down. It's okay if you fall down a hundred times or even a thousand times. What matters is whether you get back up. A winner is someone who learns from these experiences and continues to stay committed to excellence.

Falling down actually provides us with the tools to become successful, whatever that means TO YOU. It also provides us with opportunities to learn and grow. If you believe in what you are doing, you must give it all you have got. The only thing that is certain is you have absolutely no chance of achieving your dream if you don't muster up with courage to try one more time - or a hundred more times if that's what's required.

No such thing as failure

The truth is there is no such thing as failure. Every action produces an outcome. It may not always be the outcome you are looking for, but it is an outcome nonetheless. If you keep an eye on the results of your actions and keep correcting what isn't working, you will eventually produce the outcome you are looking for. Persistence is so powerful that ultimately failure cannot exist in its presence.

NEVER, EVER GIVE UP!

NEVER!

So many successful people have sad tales to tell about how they faced obstacle after obstacle in life. It is helpful you note this now while you are still young and on the brink of creating an amazing life for yourself.

On the way to success you are going to make mistakes - lots of them - and it's OKAY! In fact failure is to be expected and embraced because that is how we learn - from making errors and learning what does and doesn't work. We all make mistakes - it's nothing to be embarrassed, anxious or nervous about.

Sure it's not fun making mistakes and feeling scared. But you know what is even scarier? It's not trying, not knowing what you could have achieved and not experiencing everything life has to offer you. Especially when the opportunity is sitting there, waiting for you to act. So be brave enough to live life to its fullest every day.

Just so you know, it is normal to doubt yourself and question your worth and abilities.

Self-confidence however comes from within – from knowing failure won't kill you. It comes from knowing you will usually get better at things with time and practice and from knowing you are special. You really are! All of these things are true so remind yourself often of these facts especially if you want to achieve great things.

When you aren't scared to do things, you open yourself and your life up to so many new experiences. You learn and understand failure isn't something to be upset about because something good comes out of every experience. Even if you don't come first or get exactly what you hoped for, you are doing something infinitely more important. And that's living and embracing life – the good, the bad and the not so pretty. When you do these things without letting fear stop you, you show courage and grow more confident every day.

So change the way you look at failure and don't let it stop you from living the life you dream about. Here are the stories of 50 inspiring individuals who did just that – refused to let failure stop them. With this courage they went on to create and live the most amazing lives.

50 FAMOUS PEOPLE WHO DIDN'T GIVE UP

1.   Thomas Edison

When he was in first grade his teachers expelled him from school and told his parents he was too stupid and mentally retarded and not suitable to receive an education. Edison spent many hours experimenting in the family garage and tried 10,000 different experiments before he came up with a solution and invented the world's first electric globe. In his lifetime he patented 1093 inventions.

2.   Albert Einstein

Einstein didn't start speaking until he was four years old. There was some concern on the part of his parents he might be somewhat backward. During his school years he showed no special aptitude because of his dislike for rigid methods of instruction and he was cited by school officials as being disruptive.

He failed the entrance exam to a university a number of times and he made his great discoveries while working by day in a low-level clerical job. Many today believe he was dyslexic and yet he is still widely considered to be one of the smartest individuals that ever lived.

3. Ray Kroc

At the age of 52 Kroc, the founder of McDonalds, mustered up enough courage in his new idea to re-mortgage his home and borrow lots of money. Despite being plagued by years of health issues, including arthritis, diabetes and losing his bladder and most of his thyroid gland, he continued to persevere and believe in himself. Today McDonalds is the second most recognisable name in the world, next to Coca Cola.

4. Colonel Sanders

At the age of 65 Colonel Sanders, a sixth grade dropout and the founder of KFC, drove across United States of America, restaurant to restaurant, often sleeping in his car, believing one day his "secret recipe" would pay off.

He was told no 1009 times before he sold his first piece of chicken. Imagine if he chose to give up after his 500th or 1000th rejection? But he didn't give up, did he?

5.   Elvis Presley

In 1954 Jimmy Denny, manager of the Grand Ole Opry, fired Elvis Presley after one performance. He told Presley: "you ain't going nowhere son. You ought to go back to driving a truck." He went on to become one of the most significant icons of the 20th century and is often referred to as the "King of Rock and Roll."

6.   Marilyn Monroe

In 1944 Emmeline Snively, director of Blue Book Modelling Agency told the modelling hopeful (then still known by her real name Norma Jean Baker): "You'd better learn secretarial work or else get married." She went on to become one of the most iconic actresses of the 1950s and is still today considered to be a major pop culture icon.

7. The Beatles

The Beatles were rejected by Decca Records in 1962. Their feedback on their ability: "We don't like their sound and guitar music is on their way out." The Beatles went on to become widely regarded as the most influential act of the rock era, selling more than 178 million albums in the United States alone.

8. Malcolm Forbes

Even though he became the editor-in-chief and publisher of Forbes magazine (a business magazine, which a portion of was reportedly sold for $300 million in 2013) Forbes failed to even make the staff of the school newspaper as an undergraduate at Princeton University.

9. Al Pacino

Pacino was rejected for the part of Michael in "The Godfather" a number of times before he eventually won the role which went on to bring his international acclaim and recognition.

10. Sylvester Stallone

Stallone was turned down a thousand times by agents and was down to his last $600 before he found a company that would produce his first film Rocky. In 1977 Stallone was nominated for two Academy Awards for *Rocky* - for Best Original Screenplay and Best Actor. He became the third man in history to receive these two nominations for the same film.

11. Arnold Schwarzenegger

Schwarzenegger was told if he wanted to succeed as an actor he better learn to speak without an accent and change his name. He went on to gain worldwide game as a Hollywood action film icon.

12. Woody Allen

The Academy Award-winning writer, producer and director flunked motion picture production at New York University and the City College of New York. He also failed English at New York University.

13. Billy Joel

Joel was denied his high school diploma due to excessive absenteeism. He ran away from home and was arrested on suspicious of burglary. The charges were dropped but a terrifying night in jail did little to help build a happy outlook on life. He attempted suicide by drinking furniture polish instead of bleach because he thought "it would taste better".

When that didn't solve his problem he committed himself to a mental ward at Meadowbrook Hospital for three weeks and quickly discovered he was quite sane. The hospital visit strengthened his resolve to make it in rock and roll. He had many more failures before he finally succeeded. To date he has sold more than 150 million albums.

14. Buddy Holly

In 1956 Holly was fired by Paul Cohen from Decca Records. Cohen called him "the biggest no-talent I have ever worked with'. Twenty years later Rolling Stone magazine named Holly, along with Chuck Berry, a major influence on rock music during the Sixties.

15. J.K Rowling

Even though her Harry Potter brand is estimated to be worth $15 billion today, Rowling was at one point in her life a depressed, divorced, penniless, single mother raising a child on her own. Twelve publishers rejected her Harry Potter manuscript.

During a Harvard commencement speech, the author outlined the importance and value of failure. In her words: "I had failed on an epic scale. An exceptionally short-lived marriage had imploded, and I was jobless, a lone parent, and as poor as it is possible to be in modern Britain, without being homeless. The fears that my parents had had for me, and that I had had for myself, had both come to pass, and by every usual standard, I was the biggest failure I knew." Coming out of this failure stronger and more determined was the key to her success. Her books went on to sell more than 400 million copies and are the best-selling book series in history.

16. Louis L'Armour

The successful author of over 100 western novels with over 320 million copies sold received 350 rejections before he made his first sale

17. Walt Disney

Disney was turned down 302 times before he got financing for his dream of creating "the happiest place on Earth", better known today as Disneyland.

18. Steve Jobs

Amazingly Steve Jobs was fired from the company he founded - Apple. He also failed with NeXT, another computer company and the Lisa computer. When Jobs later returned to Apple, he led the business to become the most profitable company in the US.

19. Steven Spielberg

Steven Spielberg was rejected both times he applied to school at University of Southern California (USC). He didn't let that rejection stop him from pursuing his dreams of being a film director. He now has a personal worth of $3 billion and the gross value from the films he has directed exceeds $9 billion. He was later awarded an honorary degree from USC.

20. Oprah Winfrey

Despite now being a multi-billionaire Oprah Winfrey endured a difficult childhood, including abuse. She was fired from one of her early television reporting jobs as "she was deemed not suitable for television." Oprah went on to become the undisputed queen of television with her talk show, "The Oprah Winfrey Show." She is also viewed as an influential figure who continues to inspire people with her positive and uplifting messages.

21. Michael Jordan

Michael Jordan is widely considered to be the greatest basketball player of all time, however he was cut from his high school varsity basketball team during his sophomore year. That only inspired him to work harder.

In his words: "I have missed more than 9000 shots in my career. I have lost almost 300 games. On 26 occasions I have been entrusted to take the game winning shot...and I missed. I have failed over and over and over again in my life and that's precisely why I succeed."

22. Jim Carrey

When Carrey was a teenager he and his family worked as janitors and lived in a tent on their aunt's lawn. The first time he got onstage to do an act at Yuk Yuk's comedy club he bombed big time. When he returned two years later he was wonderful. The now famous comedian and actor went on to star in many successful films and reportedly has a net worth of $150 million.

23. Burt Reynolds

In 1959 Reynolds was told by a Universal Pictures executive he had no talent. He went on to become a famous American actor, director and producer, starring in many television series and films. He also won two Golden Globe Awards, one for Best Actor in a Television Series Musical or Comedy and another for Best Supporting Actor - Motion Picture.

24. Lucille Ball

In 1927 Ball was told by the head instructor of John Murray Anderson Drama School: "Try any other profession. Any other." She went on to become a much-loved American actress and comedian, starring in numerous self-produced sitcoms including *I Love Lucy* and *The Lucy Show.*

25. Liv Ullman

The two-time Academy Award nominee failed an audition for the state theatre school in Norway. The judges told her she had no talent.

26. Clint Eastwood

In 1959 a Universal Pictures executive told Eastwood he had a chip on his tooth, his Adam's apple sticks out too far and he talks too slow. He went on to contribute to over 50 films as a famous American actor, film director, producer and composer, earning considerable critical praise.

27. Sidney Poitier

After his first audition, Poitier was told by the casting director, "Why don't you stop wasting people's time and go out and become a dishwasher or something?" Poitier vowed to show him that he could make it and went on to become the first African-American to win an Academy Award for Best Actor.

28. Madonna

Before becoming Madonna the now world-famous singer was Madonna Louise Ciccone. Her mother died of breast cancer when she was only five years old and she later dropped out of college to move to New York. There she worked odd jobs to pay her rent including waitressing, dancing and working as a nude model. She was fired from her jobs at Dunkin Donuts and as a hat check woman at the Russian Tea Room.

Still she never gave up her dream to sing and she succeeded. Madonna has sold more than 300 million albums worldwide and is recognized as the best-selling female recording artist of all time by Guinness World Records.

29. Stephen King

King was raised in poverty and grew up as a paranoid, troubled child. When he was two years old his father left his family by pretending he was going to buy a packet of cigarettes. King was addicted to drugs and alcohol that he used to cope with the unhappiness he felt in his life. His first book, Carrie was rejected 30 times and he proceeded to throw it in the trash.

It was his wife who retrieved it from the trash and encouraged him to try again. He eventually went on to publish 54 novels and nearly 200 short stories. His books have sold more than 350 million copies, many of which have been adapted into films, miniseries, TV shows and comic books.

30. Alexander Bell

When Bell invented the telephone in 1876, President Rutherford Hayes said: "That's an amazing invention but who would ever want to use one of them?"

31. Ludwig Van Beethoven

Even though this German composer is considered to be the most famous and influential of all composers his music teacher once said of Beethoven "as a composer, he is hopeless." By his late twenties his hearing began to deteriorate and by the last decade of his life he was almost totally deaf but still be continued to compose. Many of his most admired works come from the last fifteen years of his life.

32. Vincent Van Gogh

During his lifetime this artist suffered from mental illness, failed relationships and committed suicide at the age of 37. He only ever sold one painting during his life so he died thinking he was a failure, when in fact he is now known as the greatest artist that ever lived. In his words: "if you hear a voice within you say 'you cannot paint' by all means paint and that voice will be silenced."

33. Edmund Hillary

In 1952 Hillary attempted to climb Mount Everest but failed. After his failed attempt he made a fist and pointed to the mountain. "Mount Everest you beat me the first time but I'll beat you the next time because you've grown all you are going to grow but I'm still growing!" One year later, on May 29, Hillary succeeded in becoming the first man to climb Mount Everest.

34. James Dyson

It took this British inventor five years and more than 5,000 failed prototypes before he finally developed the world's first bagless vacuum cleaner. Then ten years later when no other manufacturers would produce his vacuum he decided to set up his own facility. Now the Dyson is the best-selling vacuum in the world and has a net worth of almost $5 billion.

35. Fred Smith

"The concept is interesting and well-formed but in order to earn better than a C the idea must be feasible." This is the comment a Yale professor wrote on the paper written by Smith, proposing a reliable overnight delivery service. FedEx, the shipping company, now has over 300,000 employees and as of 2015 revenue of over $47 billion dollars.

36. Mary Kay Ash

Mary Kay Ash had a life filled with struggles before building her cosmetics company into a multi-billion empire. She sold books door to door while her husband served in World War 2 and when he returned from duty they divorced. Ash was left with three children at a time when there was still a real stigma about being divorced. She married again and planned a new business with her new husband but he died one month prior to the launch.

One month later, at age 45 and with a $5,000 investment from her oldest son, Ash finally launched her business Mary Kay Cosmetics. It now has 300 million independent salespeople selling more than 200 products in 35 countries and a wholesale annual revenue of over $3 billion.

37. Bill Gates

Bill Gates, currently the richest man in the world (worth $76.6 billion in 2016), didn't always seemed destined for success. He was a Harvard school dropout and his first business Traf-O-Data was a true failure. However, skill and a passion for computer programming kept him going and he later created the global empire called Microsoft. In his own words: "Its fine to celebrate success but it is more important to heed the lessons of failure."

38. Wilma Rudolph

At the age of 4 Rudolph contracted double pneumonia and scarlet fever, leaving her with her left leg paralysed. Her mother was told she would never walk again. At age 9 she removed her metal brace and by age 13 she had developed a rhythmic walk. That same year she decided to become a runner. She entered every race and came in last. Everyone told her to quit but she kept on running until one day she eventually won a race. From then on she won every race and went on to win three Olympic gold medals.

39. Jack Andraka

When Andraka was 15 he has a crazy idea to create a diagnostic test for Pancreatic Cancer that was better than the tests developed by scientists, research labs and billion dollar pharmaceutical companies. Jack wrote a proposal that was rejected by 199 research labs. Thankfully the 200th research lab — at Johns Hopkins University in Baltimore — accepted him and he went on to develop a Pancreatic Cancer test that was 100 times better and 26,000 times less expensive than the current test. It has since saved thousands of lives.

40. Theodor Seuss Geisel

There is a good chance you have read at least one of Dr. Seuss's books. His books, including The Cat in the Hat and Green Eggs and Ham have sold over 600 million copies and been translated into more than 20 languages. Yet Dr. Seuss' first book To Think I Saw It On Mulberry Street was rejected by 27 different publishers before he finally found someone who agreed to publish it.

41. Jack Canfield

Canfield was rejected by 144 publishers before he finally found a publisher for his book, *Chicken Soup for the Soul*. When Jack told the publisher his goal was to sell 1.5 million books in the first 18 months, the publisher laughed and said he'd be lucky to sell 20,000. That first book sold more than 8 million copies in America and 10 million copies around the world and this book brand is now worth $1 Billion.

42. Stan Smith

Smith is a former world number one American tennis player and two-time Grand Slam singles champion but it didn't always seem as if he would succeed in this sport. As a kid he tried to get a job as a ballboy but he was turned down because the organisers thought he was too clumsy and unco-ordinated. He later won eight Davis Cups.

43. Charles Schultz

Even though he is now famous for his Peanuts comic strip, Schultz had every cartoon he submitted rejected by his high school yearbook staff. Even after high school, the cartoonist didn't have much luck, after applying and being rejected for a position working with Walt Disney. He is now widely regarded as one of the most influential cartoonists of all time and is cited as a major influence by many later cartoonists.

44. Babe Ruth

This American professional baseball player is well known for his impressive home run record - 714 homeruns during his career. But it came with a pretty big price tag - 1330 strikeouts in total. For decades he held this strikeout record and when asked to explain he simply said, "Every strike brings me closer to the next home run."

45. R.H Macy

Even though his department store chain is now super successful, with almost 800 stores around the U.S, Macy didn't always have it easy. Macy actually started four retail dry goods stores, which were all failed businesses. But he learnt from his mistakes and over time his new business grew.

46. Abraham Lincoln

Today Lincoln is remembered as one of the America's greatest leaders but he too had his own fair share of failures. For starters in his youth he went to war as a captain but was discharged from this command and re-enlisted as a private, which is the lowest of all military positions.

Some of his neighbours and family members thought he was lazy for all his "reading, scribbling, and writing" and believed he did it to avoid manual labour. He started numerous businesses which failed and was defeated in many times in his run for public office before finally becoming the 16th US President.

47. Charles Darwin

This renowned scientist, who is best known for establishing that all species of life have descended over time from common ancestors, wasn't always considered smart. He gave up on having a medical career and was often reprimanded by his father for being lazy and too dreamy. Darwin himself wrote, *"I was considered by all my masters and my father, a very ordinary boy, rather below the common standard of intellect."* Today Darwin is well-known for his scientific studies.

48. Chester Carlson

After seven long years of rejections a tiny business called Haloid Company purchased the rights to this inventor's electrostatic paper-copying process. Haloid later became Xerox Corporation. For years it seemed this was an invention nobody wanted yet because of Carlson's commitment to his dream, the photo-copier eventually became a commonplace, essential piece of office equipment.

49. Akio Mortia

The name of this businessman may not ring a bell but his company will - Sony. Their first product was an electric rice cooker that never even worked properly - it either produced undercooked or overcooked rice. After selling only 100 units they moved on from this failure and went on create a multi-billion dollar company providing consumer electronics, video games and entertainment goods.

50. Nick Woodman

After finishing school Woodman started two companies that failed. The first was a website selling electronic goods and the second was Funbug, a gaming and marketing platform that gave users the chance to win cash prizes. Funbug was back by $3.9 million from investors and all of that money was lost.

After his second business failure Woodman took an extended surfing trip and realised he wanted to take videos while he was surfing. That led to his next idea - cameras that make it easy for people to video while participating in activities.

Woodman and his future wife financed the business by selling shell necklaces they bought in Bali ($1.90) out of the trunk of their car to raise money for Nick's business (they sold the necklaces for $60). His mother also loaned him $35000 and finally GoPro was launched. The company is now worth $1 billion.

EIGHT TIPS TO DEVELOPING PERSISTENCE

So now that you know most successful people have struggled on their road to fame, fortune or happiness, it's important you recognise you too will have struggles in your life. You 100% will so expect it and plan for it.

To succeed you are going to have to develop the habit of persistence. It's a habit which means even if you feel like you don't have this skill just now, you don't need to worry. It can be developed. Just like you learned to read and learned to do math you can also learn the skill of persistence.

Here are some simple tips which will help you develop this habit if you don't feel like you have mastered it just yet. The good news is these tips don't require from you great intelligence or education but they do require from you ACTION.

1.   Get support.

Not only do you deserve to be around people who are supportive of your goals, at times you may depend on it.

2. Intentionally choose to avoid negative influences.

Negative people will only drag you down.

3. Identify any counterproductive thoughts and habits you may already have.

Once you have done this, you can work out how you can dispose of them.

4. Live and eat healthily.

Energy and stamina are a must for persistence. You need them for focus, strength, optimism, self-confidence and clarity.

5. When getting advice, make sure you consider the source.

Are you seeking advice from someone with the right know-how? Are they lifting you up or pulling you down?

6.   Avoid excuses.

We are all guilty from time to time of creating
convenient alibis for why something won't work. It
is important however to be honest with ourselves.
Recognise an excuse for what it is - just an excuse -
and do not make them a way of life.

7. Willingly forgive yourself and others.

Carrying around the emotions of hatred, anger or
disappointment is toxic to your spirt of persistence.

Take reasonable risks. Without risk there is no
reward. If you continually avoid risks then you avoid
success at the same time.

8.   Finally never, ever give up!

Famous Words

When you get into a tight place and everything goes against you, until it seems as though you could not hold on a minute longer, never give up then, for that is just the place and time that the tide will turn.
Harriet Beecher Stowe.

The depth of darkness to which you descend and still live is an exact measure of the height to which you can aspire to reach. *Lauren Van du Post*

Over every mountain there is a path, although it may not be seen from the valley. *James Rogers*

IN CONCLUSION

Now that this book is over, there's a good chance you may think the advice was great but you still put it aside to go and live your life, exactly as you please. And by all means, that is fine. You are entitled to ignore the advice. There is no pressure from me to take any of it on board.

All I hope for is that a seed of strength has been planted. That you now know and understand your whole future is ahead of you. You truly can be whoever you want to be. Take some time to reflect on where you want to go. Life is as short as it is long. Feel free to break the rules. Forgive quickly, love truly, laugh freely and never regret anything that made you smile or happy.

Life is supposed to be good. Life is supposed to be embraced. You don't want to look back at your past with a wistful sigh and wish you had lived more, danced more or enjoyed more experiences outside your comfort zone.

So be brave! Seize the day! Don't be so afraid you don't even have the guts to try new things. What are you waiting for? Until you are *old enough? Seriously?* This is your time to begin dreaming big and taking action now! Even little steps are fine.

Your teen years are a unique experience in that you have to socialize with people you may prefer not to see. Sometimes you get judged on your appearance (even though it's the inside that counts) and your heart may get broken multiple times (by people who don't even deserve your heart to begin with).

While your teen years may change you, it isn't an overnight dramatic evolution like in the movies. It's gradual, natural and comes with time. As you grow older and wiser, you will gain more and more skills that make you feel more equipped to take on the world.

Unfortunately you can't start the next chapter of your life if you keep re-reading the last one. So find out what's important to you. Are you heading in the right direction? There's a good chance your priorities and path will change as you get older but that's okay. No one expects an 18 year old to remain the same when they are 25 or 35. Adjust your sails and change your course if and when necessary.

Remember life rarely turns out the way we expect it to but every struggle shapes us into the person we are today. Be thankful for the hard times, for they only made you stronger. Finally, know that in the end we only regret the chances we didn't take.

In the end, it's not the years in your life that count. It's the life in your years. Abraham Lincoln,

The most important thing is to enjoy your life - to be happy - it's all that matters. Audrey Hepburn.

OTHER BOOKS BY FRANCES VIDAKOVIC

Fiction

- *Before I Die: A Pact*

- *Just A Little Break*

- *Pretty Mansnatchers*

- *Enchanted Island*

Non-Fiction

- *Happy Thoughts: 200 Inspiring Quotes Explained for Kids and Teens*

- *The Smart Kids Guide to Everything*

- *Create a Life You Love*

- *They Say I'm Special: 100Tips for Raising a Happy and Resilient Child with Special Needs*

- *When He's A Keeper: But You Feel Like Throwing Him Away*

- *Croatian Princess: A Collection of Musings*

For more information visit her author page on Amazon or website at www.inspiringlifedreams.com.

66964048R00093

Made in the USA
Middletown, DE
16 March 2018